Nothing Wasted

by

RENEE BRADFORD

Published by TDR Brands International
& Legacy Publishing Coordinators

Printed in the United States of America

First Printing: 2022

ISBN: 978-1-947574-61-8

Published By: TDR Brands International & Legacy Publishing Coordinators

Dedication

This book is dedicated to anyone who's ever felt unloved, forgotten, or abandoned.

Your journey may not look like what you expected, or with the people you expected.

Know that God is intentional, and he orchestrated the right people in your path for you to accomplish your mission and your purpose.

Sometimes the very people that we start with or encounter on our journey are not equipped to take the entire journey with us. The beauty is that God already knew that - and because He works all things together for good, He has placed other people and circumstances in your life to provide you with everything you need or ever needed.

My goal in sharing my story and writing this book is to encourage you to take another look and see the blessings and people carefully and thoughtfully placed by the hand of God to fill those needs and take you through your journey.

Nothing Wasted, nothing you experience is ever Wasted.

Jeremiah 29:11
For I know the plans I have for you, declares the Lord, plans to prosper you and not to harm you, plans to give you hope and a future.

Contents

Introduction

"Nobody wants you. I tried…I talked to everybody. Nobody wants you.".

My brother Russell and I sat—shocked--in the back of my father's taxicab, listening but unable to believe what we were hearing.

"I can't do this. I can't take care of you two anymore, and no one wants you. I'm taking you to a place where they can take care of you."

We had been living with our dad and his girlfriend for months until we had been evicted a few days prior. Russell and I were in grade school.

"What are you talking about, 'You can't do this?' Somebody wants us!" Russell shouted.

"I checked with everybody. Nobody wants to take you."

I felt the burn in my eyes as the tears began. I could see Russell's eyes welling up, too. "What about Grandma? What about our godmother? What about Ms. Banks? What about…"

"I said I asked everybody! They all said they can't take care of you!"

Nobody. Wants. You. The earth had just opened under us, and all we could do was howl and scream and cry.

I don't know how my father could live with giving his children away; his son and daughter crying their guts out in the back of his taxicab…heaving, racking sobs, wailing at the idea that nobody wants us. But somehow, he just kept driving to the Social Services Office.

In that cab, on that day, I discovered purpose. I realized that the world I was supposed to know, with a mother and father and family, was not going to happen for Russell and me. Everything I thought I knew was now gone, and I was going to have to take control of my life. I recognized in that moment that I could have no control over what other people do, and while I didn't know why this happened, and I really didn't care, what I cared about most was making sure this would stop right here. I vowed to make sure this never happened to me or anyone in my life again. That's what I signed up for in that moment. Even at that age, I had the agency of mind to tell myself to face forward and figure out how to do it. Why my mother was sick, why my father couldn't do it anymore, why nobody wanted me weren't important. Somehow I reasoned that having that information wasn't going to help me to keep my vow.

We cried and we cried. It seemed like a lifetime of tears, like we would never be able to stop, and we would be sobbing and hollering forever and ever. I looked at Russell's bawling face, and I looked at the back of my father's head, and suddenly I took a hard breath in, like after a sucker punch, and I stopped crying. Russell kept crying and screaming about how this was crazy and he couldn't believe no one wanted us, but I sucked in a deep breath, wiped my face, and told my brother to stop crying. I was done with crying.

I realized that this day, this shifting, this abandonment--whatever it was--was going to happen and I couldn't do a thing about it. At the same moment, I knew that somehow I could make sure that nothing like this would ever happen to us again. Somehow I had to figure out what I had to do to make sure that I would never again be this helpless.

My story is one of miracles. There have been many traumatic circumstances, many trials, but living life with purpose has made me a happy woman. My purpose has changed, but the power of purpose is awesome (and I'm using the real meaning of the word: "inspiring an overwhelming feeling of reverence." Growing from "I will never let this happen again" to "What does God want me to do?" has not lessened my energy or my resolve.

I trust God. He has provided, continues to provide, and as long as I put my feet to the floor and put one foot in front of the other, we will always have our needs met.

Some days I think about this life and I think, "Why did you do those things? Look how much you lost, look at what you went through, put yourself and your family through."

Then I reflect and I tell myself, "You would never know God the way you know Him now if you hadn't gone through what you had to go through." And how much is that worth?

My husband Dwayne and I have been married for 36 years. We raised two children and a nephew who came to live with us.

We have always had the fabulous blessing of taking care of our relatives, his and mine. My grandmother, my cousin (it's been hard to keep count), but I believe there were eight people in this big beautiful home while we were raising the children, and I could not have been more blessed.

My challenges today are of the heart. When I hear people say they love me, there's still a wall around my heart. I know the ones who mean it are being true, but it doesn't quite penetrate the wall. It is coming down slowly--so slowly--but I've had to learn that it's

God's timing, not mine.

I am a busy woman, and I have always been busy. My grandmother used to say, "If you want something done, give it to a busy person." God has given me the gift of being not just busy, but efficient. In my life as a mother, I have been the most efficient, joyous person I know. When I am in it, I am *in it*, and then I rest - because I have to. Efficiency with a purpose is not just "busy." Being empowered by God is not just "busy." And when I learned to rest, I learned to rest my mind. Mental rest is peace.

My older daughter Courtney is a lawyer. She attended Columbia University for undergrad and then graduated from Columbia University Law School. My younger daughter Dominique, who has been diagnosed with receptive expressive language disorder, has a career as a certified nursing assistant. We did not know if she could handle the schooling, but she was making straight As. She first learned how to care for people by caring for two of her grandmothers in our home.

When my nephew came to live with us, he was in the seventh grade and had difficulty reading. My husband worked with him; he had him read aloud and kept him engaged in his schoolwork. After graduating high school, he attended Morehouse College and then Morehouse School of Medicine. Today he is an ophthalmologist on staff at the University of Kentucky.

We did not do these things. God runs my house. At best, we have been blessed to be vessels for God's work.

While we managed this house full of people, this house full of tasks, my husband Dwayne started a restaurant business. We tried, we prayed, but we lost every dime we had in that business. We moved on, and we still move on, together.

God has allowed me to be in places and to go through things so I could tell this story of triumph over tragedy, of grace over trial. God has shown up in some unexplainable way at every step of my journey. It's my privilege to put my story before you.

I never wanted to tell my story – I never wanted people to feel sorry for me because I don't need it. I have been a sister on a mission, and at the end of the day, I'm good. Who has time to be a victim? Why open that door?

Because this journey has uncovered God's grace and mercy in my life, and I feel called to share that with anyone who wants to know. I hope you can relate my experiences to some of your and see how trauma and tragedy can be transformed into goodness and grace. I hope I can help some of you find the blessing that comes out of your pain.

God works all things for the good of those who are called according to His purpose. – Romans 8:28

View from the 14th Floor

CHAPTER ONE

My mother was the center of my childhood. My beautiful, statuesque, well-spoken, perfect mother. She was dignified. There was never a hair or a word out of place. She was impeccable in dress, in manner, in style. A true gracious lady. I hope I continue to live up to that part of her.

We lived in the projects – Marble Hill Houses in the Bronx, 14th floor. My brother Russell and I shared a bedroom when we were little, and every morning when we woke up, there were our clothes, our outfits, neatly laid out and ready for us. Our mother was always a sharp dresser, and so were we. It was all there – from socks and underwear to topcoat in the winter. My mother took pride in looking great and having her children look better. We lived *in* the projects, but we were not *of* the projects.

To this day, I love fashion the way my mother did. I love jewelry, and like my mother, I like my hair to stay in place. Like many New York women, I enjoy putting outfits together. Hair, fashion, jewelry, everything started with how my mother raised me.

Other kids who packed a lunch for school took a sandwich and a cookie in a brown paper bag. My mother sent us out with a meal in casserole dishes. Not Tupperware – real ceramic casserole dishes with hot food. It didn't matter if we had franks and beans, it was in a casserole dish.

People in our neighborhood would make comments and we heard them: "Who do they think they are?" We didn't care; my mother made sure that we knew who we were. She wanted us to experience all the good things life and New York City had to offer. If something was happening that was appropriate for two little kids, my mother, my brother Russell, and I were there. Radio City Music Hall, the Ice Capades, museums, we got to see and do it all. And those experiences gave me my love of the arts and theater.

We had an image to portray, my mother, my brother, and me: the Beautiful Black Family. We were looking perfect at all times.

I was a curious child, and a talker. The only thing I ever got into trouble for in school was being talkative. The comment section of every report card was the same: "Renee is a wonderful student. She talks too much." I always had something to say about something, and like everything in our lives, my mother wanted to maximize that. She had altered my birth certificate so that I could start kindergarten early! I can hear her now, "Tell them you're five!" She wanted me to have it all, and as soon as possible. And no one ever questioned my age because I was tall, talkative, and smart.

She was a single parent because my father was absent. He was alive, my parents were married, but he showed up when he showed up. When The Temptations sang, "Papa Was A Rolling Stone," they were singing about my father. Mom was 15 and Dad was 17 when she got pregnant with Russell, and I followed 13 months after. Talk about babies having babies! In those days, if you got pregnant, you got married. They dated in high school and then bam! My dad, Russell Burke, Jr., came from a good family, so I'm sure they held his feet to the fire.

But throughout our childhood, Dad just wasn't there. Now and then this tall, drop-dead handsome man would show up, we'd say

"Hi, Dad," and then he would disappear. My mother didn't speak of him when he was gone. We lived our lives and she did everything. She ran the show; every day we had a purpose, there was a plan, and we went about our business.

I don't think ill of my dad, even the way he was in those days. He wasn't ready to be a husband or a father. He didn't want to be part of my mother's plan. He just wanted to be out there in the world, and he had seen that same behavior in his father. It was passed from generation to generation, or inherited in the DNA – fathers not being present in the lives of their children. There was no pretense, it wasn't hidden. He wasn't there; he'd show up, then he wasn't there.

My mother needed some time to herself, of course, and time to go out, so we would go to visit her mother, my grandmother Leila. Grandma Leila was domineering, and if my mother was a director, Leila was a boss. I'm sure that's a big part of the reason Mom and Dad got married when they did. Leila had three children: my aunt Mary, my uncle Wally, and my mother. I have no idea what went on in their house when my mother was growing up, but I later learned that my aunt Mary suffered from paranoid schizophrenia, Uncle Wally had serious drug issues and, ultimately, was murdered.

My mother was the one who had it together.

As I said, my mother always looked perfect, and part of that image was that anyone she was seen with had to look good. She dated an extremely handsome man for quite a while. His name, as far as we knew, was Red. He was larger than life, and he always treated Russell and me well. I was a kid, what did I know?

Red took us shopping – Mom only shopped at places like Bloomingdales and Macy's. We were all decked out: my mother and I in rabbit fur, Russell dressed to kill, it was fantastic! It was later on when I learned, and I'm sure it was Leila who told me, that

Red was a drug dealer. He wasn't a lowlife street dealer, no sir! Red was one of the biggest drug kingpins in New York City.

He and my mother fit perfectly because men like that wanted a woman with *image*. Someone who always looked good, would never embarrass him, and turned heads. My mother fit the bill. She was a perpetual ladylike stunner, and she never came out of the image. Never.

As Russell and I got to be around nine or ten, I started to see the seams in my mother's perfect image. She began acting differently toward my brother. Now, Russell Burke III was no saint. He was what you would call "mischievous."

One Christmas, Russell found where my mother had hidden the presents. They hadn't been wrapped yet, and he was sitting in my mother's room playing with them when two things happened: my mother caught him, and I found out that there was no Santa Claus. I don't know who ended up hurting more. Russell's mission in life was to pick at me. He would pick at me, tease me, and I would yell, "STOP IT, RUSSELL! LEAVE ME ALONE!" and he loved it.

My mother had always been disciplined, and she disciplined us when we needed it, but the way she started acting toward Russell was moving in the direction of abuse. Screaming at him, hitting him – not beatings, but frequent "smacking;" Russell was exasperating, but as her treatment of him got worse, that wasn't an excuse anymore.

One weekend, as we frequently did, we went to my grandma Leila's apartment. My mother had given us the usual lecture about what not to say: don't talk about your father, don't talk about money, basically don't give Leila any ammunition.

Leila liked the party life. When we stayed with her, she would take us to a bar near her house in Spanish Harlem and put us in a booth while she hung out with her friends. The people at the bar knew us; they would give us sodas and we were cool. Like every bar, there was a jukebox, and that jukebox had every popular song on it. I learned them all. I would sit and sing in that booth, from Billy Paul's "Me and Mrs. Jones" to "Rock Steady" by Aretha Franklin. They played those songs over and over, and I learned every song from that era. I still have a deep love for R&B, good old soul music that you would hear in a bar. I doubt if my mother even knew that Leila was taking us to that bar.

One beautiful day, we were at the window of Leila's 12th floor apartment in Spanish Harlem. The sun was streaming in, there was probably a breeze coming up from the street, and I heard someone screaming and hollering from down on the curb. I looked out and saw an ambulance parked in front of Leila's building, and two men in white uniforms were struggling with someone--a woman who was screaming bloody murder as they tried to get a straitjacket on her.

It was my mother, and my life wasn't going to be perfect anymore.

Guardian Angels

CHAPTER TWO

It would be many years before I would see my mother again. To this day I don't know how it happened, what triggered the event of her being taken away. They took her, literally, kicking and screaming, and that was that.

No one ever said "mental hospital" or "institution." That's where she was, but we didn't know. At some point, I heard the phrase "nervous breakdown," but at that age, I never put it together. We were told, "Your mom is sick; she's going to be in the hospital for a while." Of course, that made sense. Sick, hospital--she'll be back, okay.

We stayed at my grandma Leila's house at first. She had a co-op apartment in a complex in Manhattan. Of course, we missed our mother and felt the loss of her presence daily. She was such a force in our lives; it was as if the earth had shifted below our feet, but kids adapt. Russell always said he hated going to our grandmother's house, but when we were there, we could always find other kids to play with. We adapted because we had to. And it was not going to be the last time our world was going to be rocked.

We were in Spanish Harlem with Leila, but we were still going to grade school next to Marble Hill.

We had had a babysitter in the Marble Hill projects--Ms. Banks--that had taken care of us and just about every other kid in the neighborhood at some time or another. Ms. Banks was a stay-at-home mother; her husband, Johnny, worked at the post office, and she had three kids of her own, but she always made room for children. We loved Ms. Banks. She was stability - we saw her every weekday ever since I could remember. She was our babysitter and like a surrogate mother to all the kids who knew her.

At some point there must have been a conversation among the grownups. I'm still not sure how and why we ended up with Ms. Banks, whether it was due to the distance so it would be easier for us to get to school, or if it was because Ms. Banks raised her hand to say we could stay there so that we would have a place to live. The latter is probably the reason.

The story, as I heard it later, was that my grandmother Leila was willing to keep us – if there was going to be some kind of money coming from somewhere. On the other hand, Ms. Banks just said she would take us with no conditions. That woman had a heart as big as the Bronx. Ms. Banks provided something Leila could never have done: a family life.

I have to point out that Ms. Banks was not a relative nor a family friend. She was respected by the people in the neighborhood and by my mother, She didn't have to take us in because she had a full house and a full life. But her heart was always open, and she loved all of the children she had in her care. Her willingness was nothing less than a miracle, and Ms. Banks was an angel in my life. I will always love that woman and her family for what she and her husband Johnny did for Russell and me, and how their children Linda, Wanda, and Johnny, Jr. shared their parents and lives with us with open arms and hearts.

And so we went to stay with Ms. Banks. We thought it would be a short-term arrangement, that we would be houseguests or visitors, but one day eased into another and then another, and over time we simply lived there. It felt good to stay in a safe and familiar place like Marble Hill. We knew the projects, we knew the children in the neighborhood, and we knew the games. Marble Hill has nine buildings surrounding a big grassy area where we used to play, although a lot of the games we played were sidewalk games. Every neighborhood in New York City has different rules for games like hopscotch and skully, and we played using Marble Hill rules.

I liked playing skully, a game played with bottlecaps on a big chalked square. The fun part was filling the bottlecaps with melted crayons to give them weight, and then shooting the caps from one position to another by flicking them with your fingers…it was simple, and it was the best.

Russell and I were just folded into the Banks family. I don't know how she did it with a husband and three kids in a two-bedroom apartment! We went where they went and did what they did. We were cared for and taken care of, and we were part of the family. We were never made to feel out of place, although, of course, out of place was exactly what we were. The Banks family could not have been better to us, but we weren't home with our mother, and all we knew was she was in a hospital. We had no idea where Dad was. Our grandma Leila was a long subway ride away. What was going on? And why was this happening?

How did this little girl cope with the loss and confusion she didn't even know she was feeling? I became fat. I became enormous. My world had turned to dust in an instant, and I must have known it could happen again. Life was a minefield and I controlled nothing

– except what I could put in my mouth.

I don't remember the weight coming on; it just became a problem finding clothes that fit. Anytime we had somewhere to go it was a major production. "What are we gonna do with Renee? What are we gonna put on her?" I wore a size ten shoe in the third grade. Today you can go online and find sizes for anyone, but back then you couldn't find clothes to fit a really overweight kid. Still, somehow Ms. Banks always found a way. I don't know if she took in adult-sized clothes or what; I only knew I had some clothes and shoes and an angel who gave me a home that wasn't my own. Ms. Banks provided normalcy in the most abnormal situation. I just felt terrible that Ms. Banks had to work so hard just to find things for me to wear.

Of course, when you're a really large kid you take some abuse, mostly from other kids, but I don't remember much of it. There was some name-calling, of course, and there was the way kids and even adults looked at you when you were obese. I remember the tone of people's voices shifting between shock and pity. I think the worst of it was when you heard them say things like, "Such a pretty face - if only she would lose some weight..." But I couldn't let it get to me. I think I was on a mission even then, trying to fill an opening that had nothing to do with food, but the food was what I had. Food was a certainty; as long as I was eating, I was okay.

And as long as I had my brother and Ms. Banks, I was okay, too.

My God, Piggly Wiggly

CHAPTER THREE

Most New Yorkers don't spend their summers in the city if they can go somewhere else. The city is hot and humid, and outside of air conditioning, there's no real escape. There are a lot of places where the sun goes down and the streets cool off for the night, but New York City is not one of those places. The heat just lingers all day and night, and it's so damp you feel like you're drinking the air instead of breathing it.

If you lived in New York City and you had family in the South, you went south for the summer. Ms. Banks had family in Manning, South Carolina, and every year the family would get ready, load up the car, and drive to Manning. And it wasn't just Ms. Banks and her family unit that went, but the New York contingent of the Banks family. I remember every day for two weeks leading up to the trip, brothers and sisters and cousins would be calling back and forth on the phone and having meetings about who would be driving, what we were taking, and what to pack to eat in the car. The night before the drive, Ms. Banks was up all night frying chicken, and Johnny Banks was packing the car. In the morning, the whole family met up to caravan down to South Carolina.

It was a long drive, but I don't remember hearing "Are we there yet?" or anything like it. We sat in the back seat of Mr. Banks' nice car, and all I could think about was eating that fried chicken wrapped in a piece of Wonder Bread, dripping with seasoned grease. I would ask for a piece of chicken, and someone would say, "Renee, you just had a piece of chicken!" It was so good, and the cooler full of deliciousness was on the floor between us, calling to me.

The trip itself was an adventure! Each restroom stop was someplace I'd never been before. We saw trees and cows and strange license plates. This was all new and exciting. But nothing got us ready for Manning, South Carolina.

Growing up in the Bronx, and going all over Manhattan with my mother, I had never seen a red dirt road in my life. Russell and I were laughing, "What's wrong with these people? They forgot to cement the streets or what?"

When we got to our destination, Ms. Banks told us we could get out of the car and go play as soon as we had said our proper "Hellos.".

Manning was country...it was truly a different world. It could have been another planet. Everybody knew everybody, people lived in houses instead of big apartment buildings, and dirt and grass was not limited to the park! In the evening, crickets sang and lightning bugs blinked in the air. There might have once been a cricket in the Bronx, but he would have died of loneliness! There was amazing freedom we could not have known in New York City. We could run and play without looking over our shoulders. We didn't have to get the "Don't look at anybody" or "Don't talk to strangers" lecture. We could talk to the neighbors and nobody worried. I couldn't believe people lived like this.

We were staying with relatives of Ms. Banks, and again we were just absorbed into the family and loved as much as anyone. But Russell and I still knew. They were wonderful to us, but they were not our people. Manning was a great experience, and I was grateful then and now. But, like everything else, we didn't belong, and it was going to end anyway.

One day, we went with Ms. Banks and some other relatives to a store called the Piggly Wiggly. We laughed so hard about that! "What is a Piggly Wiggly?" Not Pathmark or Food Emporium, but PIGGLY WIGGLY! Oh my goodness. The store even had a picture of a smiling pig wearing a little hat – he looked like Porky Pig – on the sign!

Inside, it was a supermarket like all supermarkets, but we kept on giggling – Piggly Wiggly!

One day while we were there, a man we didn't know was speaking with Ms. Banks. He came up to us and started staring at Russell and me. We were with Ms. Banks' family, and this man started a conversation with Ms. Banks. He introduced himself as Bobby, and he kept looking at Russell and me, and then he asked her who we were. She said our names: Renee and Russell Burke! And he said we were family!

What was going on? Who was this man, and how did he know us?

Bobby said that we were his niece and nephew.

Uncle Bobby, who we did not know and first met in the Piggly Wiggly in Manning, South Carolina, was my father's brother and he lived in Manning, South Carolina. It had to be a miracle.

"You are my family," he said to us, smiling. "Please bring them over," he told Ms. Banks.

"Oh my God, we have family!" As grateful as we were for all that Ms. Banks was doing for us, we had been so disconnected, so adrift, and now we were so excited. Here was Uncle Bobby, a real relative, an anchor. And we found each other, by God's grace, in a Piggly

Wiggly in Manning, South Carolina.

We visited with Uncle Bobby and Aunt Loretta. Bobby was what one might call a "dapper gentleman." He was a wonderful husband and father, and Loretta matched him perfectly. They had two grown children, Barbette and Wayne, whom we would meet later. I'm still close to my cousin Barbette and her husband Curtis.

Then there was another surprise: Bobby's parents were living there--my father's grandparents. We had great-grandparents!

I am sure there were many questions asked between my aunt and uncle and the Banks family, like what were we doing with them in the first place. Where was Russell, my dad, in all this? But those conversations didn't take place in our presence. I am so thankful today that the adults in that situation never once had a conversation in front of us that would make us feel awkward or ashamed. We were protected, kept safe by the families around us. Although, of course, I couldn't see it then.

We spent a lot of time that summer with Uncle Bobby. Russell locked onto him and I loved him, too. It was a beautiful thing, finding our family. The days started to get shorter, and we had to go back to New York City and back to school, but maybe the ground beneath us was a little bit firmer knowing we had people.

As life went on, Russell would visit Uncle Bobby and Aunt Loretta fairly often, once for a whole summer. They loved him like he was their own child, and Russell adored them and cherished that relationship.

One day we came home from school and Ms. Banks said she wanted to talk to us.

"You know I love you two, and I always want you here," she began. "We found your father."

"Huh? What?"

"We found your father, and he's coming to get you. I told him you two could stay here if it was a problem for him, and he said no, he would come and get you."

Somebody, probably Uncle Bobby, maybe others in the Burke family, must have had words with my father, maybe shamed him, maybe put the fear of the Lord into him, I don't know and never will. But suddenly he had reappeared and he was coming to get us. And now this man, who I had only seen a handful of times and whose arrival was always just a prelude to leaving, was going to be a father to us. I suppose I should have been a little nervous or afraid, but I wasn't. This was just going to be another turn on a very rocky road.

Nobody Wants You

CHAPTER FOUR

It was only about an hour later when my father pulled up to Ms. Banks' building. It was a whirlwind from the moment he rang the bell, but I was ready. Russell may have been upset, he might have been torn up, but at ten years old I wasn't exactly checking in about feelings with my 12-year-old brother. This was sudden--nothing about our lives was normal--and I had learned to roll with it no matter what.

So this tall, handsome man comes in, introduces himself to Ms. Banks, says "Thank you" as he swooped us away, and we were out. We got in the car, my father's taxicab. Dad was in the front seat and Russell and I were in the back. My father told us we would be living with him and his girlfriend. They had an apartment near Yankee Stadium, so it wasn't a very long drive; up one hill and down the other side. My father carried our bags as we rode up to the apartment in the elevator. Then, right before we went in the door, he said, "Oh, by the way, you have a sister" just as matter-of-fact as if he was saying we were having hamburgers for supper.

A wave of indescribable joy came over me. I have a sister? I have a sister! My father unlocked the door, and this adorable three-year-old bundle with two little afro-puffs came running to the door. It was immediate love between the three of us kids, love beyond understanding. I can close my eyes today and that thrill of delight comes back instantly. I had a sister!

My little sister, Mikole, was filled with life's energy and, like me, she never ran out of words. Russell and I both took to her instantly and she became the center of our world. Mikole's mother and our father's girlfriend, Elaine, did her best to make a home for all of us. Elaine made us a part of her extended family, as she also had siblings with children in New York City. Her biggest challenge, I think, was my father. A rolling stone gathers no moss, and Russell Banks, Jr. could not maintain an emotional connection or cope with any responsibility. I was a happy child, but even then I believe I could feel the strain of us being in the home. I distinctly remember being scared the minute I heard the door unlock and my father's heavy footsteps on the hardwood floors of the apartment. Elaine did what she could given the impossible circumstance of living with my father, managing a relationship with him, and going from one child to three.

One thing she did was help my father provide me with one great blessing.

When we first came to live with them, my father looked at me and said, "Uh-uh, you too fat and I am not having this." My father, with a lot of help from Elaine, put me on a severely restricted diet. He let everybody know what Renee was not allowed to have. I drank Tab instead of Coke. Sugar no longer existed for me, and somehow I lost all the weight I had gained. I never cheated because it was always important to me to do as I was told. I didn't sneak food. If my dad said "no," then it was no.

Within one year, the excess pounds were gone and I was at a healthy weight. It was a lot more important to other people than it was to me at the time, but I am grateful that being large stopped being an issue and I could wear normal clothes like other kids.

My father was tough--strict and handy with the strap. Anytime something was broken or even out of place, his question was, "Who broke this?" or "Who moved this?" Neither Russell nor I answered, so we both got beatings. I found out later it was pretty much always Russell, but he never took one for the team. He did not confess and we got beaten together. Dad thought that hitting was the way to be a father. He just didn't know.

We couldn't have been there a year when the next rumble arrived in our life of earthquakes. Russell and I shared a small bedroom just off the kitchen, which was the hub of conversation. One night, Russell overheard a word he didn't know, and told me he had heard Dad and Elaine use the word "eviction." There was a dictionary in the apartment, so Russell looked it up: "to put a tenant out by legal process." Uh oh.

"Whatever," I said to Russell.

"We are gonna lose our home!" Russell whispered.

"Whatever," I repeated. Lose our home? We had already lost every home we had known. I wasn't going to get upset over this or anything else. It seemed like everything that was ever going to happen to us had already happened, so what was one more thing? We had already lived like little Bedouins, folding our tents as needed. If this came to pass, we'd go somewhere else.

We were still going to school in Marble Hill, so each morning we took two buses to school, and every afternoon we took two buses back. One day, a couple of weeks after Russell heard that word, we were riding the bus home and someone must have had a boombox on the bus. I heard a song I had learned and loved back in that East Harlem bar, a song by Harold Melvin and the Blue Notes. It was the powerful, expressive voice of Teddy Pendergrass soul-shouting *"Losin' your money, 'bout to lose your home...Bad Luck! That's what you got, that's what you got!"* I think I was still singing it when we walked down the hill and saw somebody's furniture out on the street in front of our building.

Of course, it was our furniture, our clothing and our stuff spread out across the front courtyard of the apartment building. To this day, I believe my father wanted the eviction to happen. His way of dealing with any kind of pressure was non-compliance followed by disappearance. Getting evicted placed him squarely on the way out of whatever his situation was.

Dad was standing there waiting for us. Elaine and Mikole were not. "We've been evicted," he said, as if we couldn't have figured that out for ourselves. "Where's our stuff?" Russell asked. "Don't worry, we'll get it." There was no moving truck, nothing. Just furniture on the sidewalk and my father wanting to get going. "Where's Mikole? Where's our sister?" "She's with her mother, and you're with me. Let's go."

Russell and I climbed into the back seat of our father's taxi and off we went to Aunt Sandra's. In my mind, Teddy P. was still singing about us.

From the first time I saw her, my aunt Sandra was the epitome of self-assurance; she was strong and sure about anything she said. If it came out of her mouth it must be a fact, because she only said things that were true and important. My aunt Sandra was strong and beautiful from the inside out. She was Afrocentric and well aware of her heritage as a Black woman, and when James Brown said *"Say it loud...I'm black and I'm proud,"* Aunt Sandra radiated that sentiment from every pore.

Larger than life in size and personality, she knew who she was.

When Aunt Sandra walked into any room she owned it and all the air in it. Without saying a word, she spoke a volume of "I am the baddest--ain't nobody better than me, finer than me, I am bad."

To this day, when I think of a woman who is in control, who is sure and positive, I think of my aunt Sandra.

Immediately, I wanted to be like her. Whatever I had to eat or drink to have what she had, I would do it! Aunt Sandra stood in herself, solid and fluid at the same time. She made you feel like you either had to follow her or get out of the way! Where my mother was beautiful and articulate, Aunt Sandra was confidence personified.

I think we were only there for a few days when it all came down. The day my father picked us up and told us he couldn't do it anymore and nobody wanted us. The ride to we didn't know where, the screaming in the back seat with my father saying over and over, "I asked everybody and nobody wants you!"

For Dad, it was just another disappearing act. For Russell, it was just too much. For me, it was the biggest decision of my life up to that point. This would never, ever, happen again. Whatever I had to do, to learn, to go through, I nor anyone I would ever be responsible for would ever be abandoned again. I was going to figure it out. That was my mission and purpose, and it would determine everything I would do from then on.

We got out of the cab outside the Social Services Office. Dad walked us in and then he was gone. That was the last time I would see him for several years. I don't know if they told him to step outside or if he simply left, but he just disappeared again. My dad.

The social worker seemed like a nice enough lady, but she just kept asking us who we could call. I looked around at the limegreen walls and the metal table and the grimy windows and kept shaking my head. My father had completely convinced us that *nobody wanted us*. The social worker acted like she couldn't believe it. I wasn't going to give her a number or a name. Why should I give her a chance to call someone and have them say they didn't want us when I already knew? Let's move on. Show me where I've got to go so I can get started on my life!

We were placed in a home called Woodycrest. It was in the Highbridge section of the Bronx, but as a kid, I thought it was in upstate New York. There were a few buildings and it reminded me of a summer camp. I was placed on the girls' side of the facility and Russell was with the boys. It was a nice enough facility: bunk beds and other kids. Cool.

In Woodycrest, I began to plan my mission. How do I create a life where I will never have to go through this again? A life where no one I love and care for will ever have to go through this? I know now that I was put in these situations so that God could mold me into the person who could fulfill this purpose. But sitting on my bed in the Woodycrest home, this was my mission, and I was going to achieve it. And luck would have nothing to do with it.

Am I an Orphan

CHAPTER FIVE

W hat would I have to do to make sure that the crazy train stops here? To make a life that doesn't feel like I'm living on the side of a volcano wondering when it was going to erupt? To ensure that my family, my someday children, would not ever have to know this kind of insecurity?

The cab ride was over, I was in a safe place, and I knew how to follow directions. All I needed now was a plan. So, what do people do to become successful at anything? Education! From that moment on when I went to class, I was 100% *on it*. I had always been a good student, but now I had *focus*. I was not going to take my eyes off the prize, which was my life, and schooling was the first step.

I was always a serious kid and I loved to read. I wasn't quite sure how education was going to do it for me, but I arrived at this understanding: uneducated people were *under*, and educated people were *standing*. I was going to be at the top of every class, and I secretly dreamed of the day when I would be free and secure.

And then there was Russell, my mischievous brother. One evening, Russell snuck over from the boys' side of the facility to where I was. "What are you doing over here?" I whispered. "You're gonna get in trouble."

"Renee," he said, "There's a payphone in this building, and I am so mad at Grandma I am going to call her and tell her off! I thought she was so nice!"

"What? Grandma Irene?" Irene was my father's mother. We hadn't spent that much time with her, but she had visited us from time to time when we lived in the projects.

"Yes, Grandma Irene! She always seemed nice to us!"

He was right. She had always been good to us when we did see her. She was kind and loving, just what you might expect a grandmother to be. And I knew that her presence, her being, was all about love and acceptance. I felt it, and I knew that anyone who encountered her felt it, too.

"I can't believe she would say she didn't want us, and I am furious," Russell went on. "I'm gonna call her up and tell her what I need to tell her. Come with me now!"

Kids can be incredibly quiet when they're doing something they are not supposed to be doing, and we were silent as we moved through the halls to the payphone. I couldn't believe that nobody caught us.

The phone booth was one of those old wooden ones with an accordion door, so once we got inside we wouldn't be heard. Grandma had one of those easy-to-remember phone numbers, and we had never forgotten it. We must have called collect – we didn't have a dime! Russell dialed her number, and we were so close in that phone booth I could hear the phone ringing on the other end. Then I heard Grandma's husband, Fletcher Crawford, say "Hello."

"Grandpa? This is Russell."

"WHAT? Russell? Russell Burke?"

"Yeah, Russell Burke. Where's my grandmother?"

I could hear Grandpa Fletcher holler, "Irene! It's Russell! I think Renee's with him! They're on the phone!" He sounded excited and happy.

This was not what we expected. I was confused for a moment, and then it dawned on me. "Russell," I said, "They didn't know!"

We hadn't called anyone because our father had told us he had asked everyone, and nobody wanted us. We hadn't even tried; we simply believed our dad. And now, with Russell's anger focused on our grandmother, we reached out.

Grandma finally got on the phone after we heard her in the background screaming and crying, thanking God and saying she was so happy we were okay. "Where are you? We have been looking everywhere for you! Tell me where you are; we'll come and get you!"

Russell was stunned. "But Daddy said you didn't want us." Our dad. Her son.

"Oh my Lord, no! Of course we want you! Where are you? Who do we need to call? We will come there tomorrow!"

She was shocked when we told her we were living in a home, basically an orphanage. She assured us again that we were wanted, and that they, along with Aunt Sandra and the rest of the family, would come and get us. The next morning, we went to see the social worker at Woodycrest to give her our grandparents' information. This time we marched into the limegreen office with the metal table. We were getting out! And our grandparents were on their way!

We were so excited about leaving Woodycrest and being with people who did care about us, who did want us and love us, and who had piled into their cars and come for us! We cried joyfully in our grandmother's arms and could not wait to go home with them.

"I'm sorry, it doesn't work like that," the social worker said. Everyone fell silent. "Your father signed you over to the State of New York. For you to be able to go, he has to come back here and sign more papers, and even that process would take time. Or," she continued, "someone would have to become your legal guardian."

"Done. Sign me up!" My grandmother was all in. "Give me the papers and let's go."

"There is a guardianship process," the social worker said. "It's similar to an adoption procedure." She described a course of action that would take six months to a year and included limited visitation, supervised day trips to Grandma's house, home visits by social services, then this, then that, and Grandma would have to go through all the legal rigamarole with the State of New York, blah blah blah.

"Can you expedite this?" Grandma asked. "Is there any way to move this along?"

"I'm afraid not. As I said, your son has signed the children over to the State. I'm sorry, but it's a long road to get them back."

My grandmother made a decision that day that had to be hard. "I will go through the guardianship process, whatever it takes," she said, "I want our custody to be safe and permanent. Once Russell and Renee come home with us, no one, including my son, is going to take these children."

I later learned that my father had, indeed, called his mother and asked if she would take us. And that she had, in fact, said that she would not. Instead, she had told him that she would take us in along with him if he was willing to come, too, carry his obligations, and stay with his kids. My father, as always, was not about to be answerable to anyone or anything and said "No." It had been the same with our aunt Sandra. Even she, with all her confidence, couldn't drum accountability into our dad.

Our father had signed us over to the State of New York, not because nobody wanted us, but because he didn't want to take responsibility for his children. And then, once again, he had vanished.

So we went through the process. We continued to live at the home and followed every direction to the letter. Incredibly, Russell was well-behaved, although he began to slip into emotional darkness. He was becoming negative to a point past pessimism. Murphy's Law was becoming Russell Burke's Law: if it can go wrong, it will go wrong, and it will happen to me. "Why me?" can be a very dangerous place at any age, but to get into that mindset as a kid, it can drag you down for a very long time. Still, he was compliant.

First were the supervised visits to our grandmother's house. Later came the unsupervised visits, then weekend stays. Meanwhile, our grandparents went through the legal fuss: paperwork, meetings, proceedings.

As for me, my mission continued. I stayed focused; I had my plan and my path. I had to get my education, and so I was an A student. I would do what I was supposed to do, and be good at whatever I did. I was going to make it, and none of this was ever going to happen to me again. Tell me what to do, and I was going to do it.

At the end of that guardianship process, we packed our things, left Woodycrest without looking back, and went home with Grandmother Irene and her husband Fletcher Crawford, whom I happily called Grandpa. I could only begin to know that this would be the beginning of the greatest blessing of all.

God's Plan

CHAPTER SIX

Past is preparation. If our father dumping us on the doorstep of Social Services was what had to happen to create our life with Grandma and Grandpa, then I'll thank my father every day for as long as I live. It was worth it all to have gained the secure and settled life we found with our grandparents.

My grandmother was a beautiful, energetic, light-brown-skinned woman who kept her hair a light reddish-brown color to complement her complexion. From the day we moved in with her, when people discovered that she was my grandmother, every last person would say, "Oh my gosh, you don't look like a grandmother! You look more like her mother."

Grandma was always full of love and compassion. Many people called her for advice or just to talk about any problems they had or difficulties they encountered. Grandma always had an encouraging word. Any room she entered, she filled with her loving energy. She exuded love, and she appreciated everyone and everything. She accepted people from all walks of life, and she just loved them because they were human.

Grandma had married her first husband, my dad's dad, the first Russell Burke, because they were in love and were having a child together. She had been very much in love with her first husband, but she ended up a single mother raising her children without a husband. She had help; if "it takes a village," then the village that helped to raise her children included her mother, who the family affectionately called "Momma Dear," and her husband, who we called "Pop-Pop." Momma Dear died when I was a little girl, but I did get to know Pop-Pop, who was a sweet loving great-grandfather. Everyone adored him.

I learned from Grandma that Momma Dear was a very strong, confident woman who raised my grandmother from a sense of strength and sureness. Even with that example, my grandmother told me that as a young girl, and even as a young woman, she was not strong at all. She said that she had accepted what was given to her, and never asked for what she wanted. She allowed people, especially her first husband, to walk all over her. Fortunately, as a grown woman (and very much as a grandmother) she came into her own, acknowledged her true self, and took charge of her life. My grandmother learned to speak up – respectfully, but to speak up nonetheless.

Grandma married Fletcher Crawford because he was a good man to marry. She told me that Grandpa Fletcher had never had children of his own. He was a military man, responsible and steady, and older than Grandma. There were no fireworks, no whirlwind romance; he could take care of her and he wanted to. He offered her security and stability, and he was confident enough to say to her, "You'll learn to love me, Irene."

Grandma hadn't been so sure about that, and by then Irene was speaking up and not about to settle for less than what she wanted and deserved.

She had learned what love felt like, and now, as a woman with two grown children, she had the freedom to seek the love she wanted. She hadn't forgotten how deeply in love she had been with her first husband.

Grandma told me later that she had been talking to her mother about Fletcher—she told her mother that Fletcher wanted to marry her, but she had said "No." She didn't love him. He was nice, responsible, respectful, a gentleman in every sense of the word, but she was not in love. There were no romantic sparks. Her practical mother said, "Girl, please. Didn't you have all the sparks with your first husband? Look where that got you-- raising two children by yourself and all alone. With a man like Fletcher, you marry him for all those reasons you stated, and then you will learn to love him, especially when you don't have to struggle, want for anything, or wonder if he will come home or if you will have a roof over your head. That, my dear, is love for real." Momma Dear and Fletcher were both right. Her kids were grown and gone, and Irene and Fletcher made a wonderful couple. And she did learn to love him, dearly.

When we came into their home, my grandmother had the experience of having raised my dad and Aunt Sandra. She learned from her mistakes and saw herself as prepared to provide a safe, warm, and loving environment for Russell and me. Grandpa had never been a parent, but he had been in the military! Put these two together, and we had what we needed most: stability and love.

Being free of Woodycrest, being free from worry, and having the support of my loving grandparents, I felt like I had what every kid needs – wings and an anchor. I could grow and fly, and maybe the world was not going to blow up anymore…although I think that worry has always been in the back of my mind.

My grandmother was a wise woman. Like most women of her era, she had some superstitions, and she often spoke in colloquialisms.

Grandma believed you should never iron on a Sunday, and that ironing was woman's work. Ironing consisted of tablecloths, sheets, napkins, and Grandpa's underwear, which were all kept in a box in the hallway closet. She insisted that the first person to enter her home on New Year's had to be a man. That was an easy one: it was always Grandpa Fletcher's little brother, the cool single uncle with a two-seater car who we called Uncle Boo-Boo.

I was raised by terms, many of which I didn't understand. I'm still working on some of them, like, "The more you cry, the less you pee." What does that mean? It took me a while to figure out "Six of one, half a dozen of the other," but I got it eventually. And "A word to the wise is sufficient" meant "if you're wise, I don't have to explain this to you."

It was a comfortable, secure home; an attached house in South Ozone Park, Queens. I had my own bedroom upstairs, and Russell lived in the renovated downstairs so he practically had his own apartment! We were never home alone--one of them was always present. My grandfather worked as a cook at Riker's Island, the famous New York City jail. He worked from 4 am to noon. My grandmother worked 9 to 5 at the Department of Health in Jamaica, Queens, not far from our home. My grandfather, with his military background, lived by the clock. He had timed the afternoon buses so "home from school" was at 4:00. "You get out of school at 3:00, you take this bus, then that bus, and that lands you at this door by 4:00." And he only had to say it once. I walked in the door every day at 4:00 on the button, and every day at that time Grandpa Fletcher was sitting in his La-Z-Boy facing the door with his eye on the wall clock. He did not play, and I did not try him. That might have made some kids feel constricted, but it made me feel cared for.

We had one phone in the house--a blue rotary dial phone. By today's standards, it took forever to call anybody because you had to dial each digit. The phone was on a nightstand in my grandparent's bedroom, and since Grandpa went to bed at 8 pm, there were no phone calls after that time. This made me extremely selective about sharing my phone number with anyone, especially boys.

My grandparents gave us structure. I was the girl, so I cooked. Every day. As with ironing, gender equality wasn't a thing in our home. Since Grandpa was a chef, he taught me the basics: how to clean, cut, and cook a chicken, how to make a stock or a gravy, boil water, set the table, clean up, and as soon as he saw that I wasn't going to blow up the kitchen or separate my fingers from my hand, he let me go to it unsupervised. He was in the next room if I needed help, but he gave me instructions and left me to figure it out, and allowed me to learn for myself. As in the military, I had my orders, and he was available for additional assistance as needed. And since my grandfather was a man of the clock, he taught me to work backward. He put the problem in front of me: dinner was to be on the table by 5 pm. Then he asked me to think about how long it took to prepare each item and consider each thing that had to occur so the food was on the table on time. I was up for the challenge. Grandpa taught by result--start with what you want to end up with and figure it out from there. I learned how to think in terms of preparation and timing. I learned how to put things together and to create. I also learned to be fearless in the kitchen because I was given the freedom to figure it all out and to experiment – within limits. To this day, cooking is how I relax, feeding is my service to others and how I show love. I found my home in the kitchen, and it is still one of my favorite places to be.

Grandpa also modeled financial responsibility for me. He lived without debt! If he couldn't afford something, he saved up or did without. He bought the house we lived in with cash when he came out of the service. He also saved money so he could buy a car every five years. He had a couple of credit cards, but on the rare occasion that he used one, he paid it off right away. He didn't teach discipline any other way, but was an example of it.

My grandmother set my bedtime: 9:00 pm, and there was no discussion about it. Figure it out, Renee: home at 4:00, dinner on the table at 5:00, homework, TV, whatever, and bed at 9:00. I knew I could do it all. Being an A student was a given; nothing was getting in the way of that. I knew my priorities and I would make it work. Give me a task and I would knock it out.

With a combination of their example and trust, my grandparents taught me to organize and to be confident in my abilities. I would not be the woman I am today without those two, and I thank God for the gift of their presence in my life every day.

I was in seventh grade--junior high--and the world started to open to me. Our school, Intermediate School #8, had some wonderful teachers who genuinely cared, and one weekend they took us on a bus trip to Washington, D.C. I stayed in a hotel for the first time— me and three of my classmates shared a room! Sightseeing was unbelievable – my mother had taken us all over New York City, but the nation's capital with a bunch of kids my age was something else.

In seventh grade, I learned that there were special classes for smart kids. The New York City school system had a junior high school program called "S.P." I asked what it was, and somebody said it stood for "Smart People." I wanted in! Being in any class that wasn't an S.P. class was a problem for me because I had to be with the Smart People.

At the end of seventh grade, our homeroom teacher, Mr. Millken, told us that we could stay together as a group for eighth grade. This was terrific news – our class was like a community! But it didn't fit the mission. I raised my hand. "Mr. Millken?"

"Yes, Renee?"

"I want to go into the S.P. class for smart people." He might have been disappointed – I was breaking up the band.

I was a serious kid. I didn't watch cartoons, I read books. Looking back, it all makes sense. During the time of life when kids play, color, and have fun, life for me and Russell was serious. From my mother being sick to realizing we didn't have a family to take care of us, no mother, no father, feeling abandoned, fun and child's play was not on the agenda. I didn't even realize until recently that fun was hard for me to the point where I had to write it on my to-do list: *Have Fun*. My grandparents had been teaching me to be confident, and one of my role models, my aunt Sandra, was the personification of self-confidence. I had the background and the examples, and when I raised my hand at that moment, I discovered that by speaking up I could take control of my destiny. My purpose joined with my growing confidence and a powerful desire to get on with my life, and I became like a freight train starting that day.

Mr. Millken asked me, "Why do you want to go into S.P.?"

There was only one answer. "Because I'm smart. And I want to be with the Smart People." There it was. I had spoken my truth. And it made me so happy because I was taking another step toward my goal to ensure that I would never again be abandoned or abandon anyone else. I didn't care what the other students thought or that I was being brave to raise my hand; all I thought about was accomplishing my mission for a life of security for me and my family.

I just knew at the end of the seventh grade where I was headed, and that either you were on my train or you had best get out of the way. I never had to say it, but from that moment I lived it. Friends, schools, boys--nothing was going to derail me or even make me pause.

I started eighth grade in the S.P. class just like that, and I loved it!

I may have known that I was on a mission for sure, but thank God I had my grandmother Irene to help guide my steps. The next step on the path was one I didn't even know I needed – it was to know more about who I was.

Because of my focus, and probably because of my pain, I didn't care at all about my physical self. I never cared about my appearance; the exterior was just like a suit of armor I couldn't take off. I don't know if I felt ugly, I just told myself it didn't matter. I didn't care when I was heavy, and I lost all the weight because somebody else told me to. Did I look good? That was none of my concern. Grandma took the lead on that one.

One morning in the early summer between seventh and eighth grade, my grandmother said, "Girl, we have got to get you some shorts."

"Uh-uh," I said. "Shorts are not gonna happen. I'm not wearing shorts."

Grandma gave me the side-eye. "Excuse you? First of all, you are not telling me what you're not doing." She crossed her arms. "Second of all, why do you not want to wear shorts?"

"I look horrible."

"What? Are you out of your ever-loving mind?" My grandmother did not mince words. "I don't know what you're talking about, but we are gonna get you some shorts, and you are going to put them on. Get yourself together – we are going shopping on Jamaica Avenue."

Those were not the days, and that was not the place or the environment, where you challenged what you were told. Whatever Grandma said was the final answer, and my grandmother had spoken. We went to the stores on Jamaica Avenue, and all the way there, Grandma kept up a steady stream of "What are you talking about, you look horrible? I can't believe you're saying this crazy stuff. We gotta get you a mirror to go with the shorts!" The whole time I was thinking, *You can buy me shorts, I'm not wearing them.* Remember, I was in junior high. No matter how good my grandparents were, I was still at that age where I thought they were mean and did not understand me at all.

We got to the store and she gave the salesman my size and told him to get me some shorts. Those were the days when stores had people that helped you get what you needed. He came back with some shorts, and Grandma pointed to the fitting room. I put them on. "Now, what's wrong?" Grandma asked me. "What's wrong with you and those shorts?"

"I look terrible!"

"You know what, girl? You don't want to be one of those women that grows up and says, 'I wish I had worn shorts when I was young.' But you're not going to be one of those people, because you are going to wear these shorts!"

Thank God she did that. Remember, I was hard-wired to follow directions. Oh, I was mad at first. I didn't want to, wasn't going to, but I did because my grandmother said I was going to wear them.

And when all the other kids were wearing shorts and I was, too, I felt normal. And my grandmother kept telling me, a little at a time, that I looked good, looked cute. She assured me about the part where I had no self-assurance, and I started to see myself a little differently. I started to see her a little differently, too.

But cute doesn't get you educated. Cute doesn't keep you from getting evicted. Cute doesn't keep you out of the orphanage. My mission was always first, although my grandparents eased my path in every way they could.

Grandma's Hand

CHAPTER SEVEN

It was still summer when Grandma told me that my great-grandparents, her mother and father, Momma Dear and Pop-Pop who lived down in Manning, South Carolina, were going to be celebrating their 60th wedding anniversary.

"So you and I are going on a trip – just us. I want you to come with me," she said. "You should go."

I remembered Manning, and the loving family I had down there, and I was so excited to be going. Just the two of us – no Russell, no Grandpa—it was a girls' trip! We packed up. Of course, she bought me at least one new outfit, and if I remember correctly, we took the train.

We talked, we ate, we were both so thrilled as the scenery whipped past us on the other side of the window. I'm sure I had a book or two with me, and the trip went by quickly.

In Manning, we were once again surrounded by family. It was so good to see Uncle Bobby and Aunt Loretta again, and Grandma stayed with me, telling me who everyone was and how they were related. She was so good about that – I would never have passed a "who's who" quiz! "That's your aunt so-and-so, that's your father's father's cousin…" I was just loving it up, sucking up the knowledge that gave me context, that filled in another blank regarding who I was.

And I also got to see again the two people who became my role models: my cousins Barbette and Curtis, who were Uncle Bobby's daughter and her husband. They were a beautiful Black married couple with two young kids, and they gave me a vision: this is what "normal" looks like! Barbette and Curtis were to me what was on the other side of my mission. Education, drive, purpose – all those things led to a regular life, what my cousins had. These were people who would not ever drop their kids off at Social Services.

Curtis and Barbette were college-educated, intelligent, and you could see their love for each other. Barbette had this big, gorgeous afro – I wouldn't compare her to Angela Davis except for the hair and the education – and they had Monica and Calvin, their two kids. They amazed me and I kept on watching them.

Now I knew what I wanted on the other side of this life. A home and a family, with nobody who would pull the rug out from under us. And I could see it right in front of me.

Barbette and Curtis didn't know I was looking at them. I still do. I got to tell them what they've meant to me this past year when they celebrated their own 50th wedding anniversary.

We returned to New York, and the life I was building had that new element – a goal. Purpose, mission, education, and knowing where I was going. Grandma was about to plug another module into my life plan: church.

"How come we got to go to church if you're not coming with us?" Russell wanted to know. Grandma came with us the first few times, but then we were expected to attend on our own.

"Are you questioning what I'm doing?" Grandma did not play

with questioning her about anything any more than Grandpa did.

"Or are you just asking to get knocked upside your head? You are going to church."

When we were younger, our mother had taken us to Saint Stephen's United Methodist Church, which was just across from Marble Hill Projects. I don't remember much about it, except that it was a mixed congregation, mostly White, but that was our church. The church Grandma had us going to was the Community Baptist Church, a Black church on the corner of 111th Avenue and 141st Street in Queens. It was called Baptist in New York, but it would be called Pentecostal anywhere else: people would speak in other tongues, dance in the Holy Spirit, passing out "slain in the Spirit." It was... lively.

I remember one Sunday morning as clearly as if it were last Sunday. The preacher got up and said, "God is your Everything. If you don't have a mother, if you don't have a father, you always have God." I never heard that message before, but that day that man was calling me. The point hit home with me immediately! Hey, that's me: no father, no mother! If God can be both a Mom and Dad, then I want and need Him. God was made for me! And God was calling me out through that preacher. I was who he was talking about and talking to. I walked up to the front and joined the church that day.

I didn't just go up for the altar call, I went all in. As far as I knew, God was performance-based, and I had to be as perfect at religion as I had to be in school or anywhere else. I took everything the same way. You want love, you have to do something. It was what I learned from my mother, my father, even Social Services. You have to produce and perform. "So God, what do you need me to do?" I absorbed myself in church.

It took a long time for me to realize how much I equated love with performance. I think I even believed that my wonderful grandparents were good to me based on how good I was. I knew how blessed or how fortunate I was, to have the home I had with them. I never wanted to disappoint them, and because of who I was, I felt like I had to be perfect, never get in trouble, make them proud of me and glad to have me around. Any shortcoming made me feel like I was missing the mark. Where my grandparents were concerned, my goal was to make sure I never disappointed them. That was the measure of anything I did. I wanted them to always be proud of the sacrifice they made to raise my brother and me. That thought never left my mind, and I stayed in that thought with every move I made. It was a weight I proudly carried, neither a burden nor sacrifice, but a privilege I proudly signed up for, although no one had ever said or implied any such thing.

As I got older, I'm sure my grandmother noticed the way I was about church, and the way I was about pleasing her and Grandpa Fletcher.

In addition to making dinner, I also ended up doing the dishes every night. Grandma said that Russell and I both had to do dishes, but Russell got a job at the New York Public Library downtown, so he was never there to take his turn at the sink. Once again, it was time to use the power of speaking up, but I also had to remember to whom I was speaking. I needed to come with a campaign, not just a complaint because complaining would be considered disrespectful.

"Grandma," I said, "We're supposed to take turns with the dishes, but Russell is never here so I'm doing the dishes every night."

"Well, Russell works. And you're a girl."

"So? He gets to do all kinds of things because he's a boy? And I get to do all kinds of chores because I'm a girl? That's not fair."

"Life," answered Grandma, "ain't fair. But go ahead, we'll listen to what you have to say."

"Okay. I shouldn't be doing all the dishes. Russell has got to do his share." They listened. And that was all.

Russell loved his job. There weren't many things that motivated him – he used to walk around all year long wearing a hood over his head like he was trying to be invisible, so nobody would notice him and maybe cause him trouble. But he did love that job.

So I went to Russell and told him the same thing. He wasn't angry or upset; he loved me and wanted to be fair to me. At this point in our lives, my brother had latched onto me as if I were his mother. Russell said, "Renee, what if I pay you to do my share?"

"Cool. Pay me." I told Grandma that Russell and I had worked it out and that he was going to pay me. She was satisfied with that. So the lesson was reinforced – you want something, do something. And speak up.

Russell did not have the same response to God, or life in general, as I did. I had my mission and my vision, and I spent no time reflecting on what had happened to us. But Russell lived in it. He didn't have a plan, because how can you have a plan when your life can be upended in the blink of an eye? He kept his head down under that hood, dwelling in the past and hoping that nothing would happen.

He thought God didn't love him; how could his life have gone the way it did if God loved him? Meanwhile, I had submerged myself into the church like it was a baptism tank. It was something I could hold on to, something I could do. By the time I was in high school, I was teaching Sunday School every week. I was so deep into the church, Russell thought I was going to become a nun. Of course, he knew that neither the Baptist church nor the Pentecostal church had nuns; it was his way of saying I was deep and very into God, church, and religion. Russell always admired that whatever I decided to do, I was all in.

At the same time, God wasn't going anywhere, and that was good. My mother was gone, my father was gone, but God would stay. I would always have God. So He had me all the way.

I received the baptism in the Holy Spirit and I was speaking in tongues in ninth grade. I traveled with a Pentecostal evangelist. Prayer was daily, fasting was regular. I went through a period where I only wore skirts. I didn't shirk any of my responsibilities at home, but on Sundays I was at church from morning till night. During the week, if the evangelist was going to preach somewhere, she would pick me up and I went. If there was a prayer meeting on a Wednesday night, I was there.

It got to the point, I learned later, where Grandpa Fletcher wanted to go to the church just to check up on me. "Nobody goes to church that much! Something is wrong," he told my grandmother, "Maybe she's just meeting a boy."

Grandma's response was indisputable. "You can't fake God," she told him. "I see how Renee behaves, how she speaks. She told us that if we didn't repent we were gonna go to Hell. She said that to us! This," she told Grandpa, "is real."

I had told them that and meant it. But there was no disrespect - I said it because I loved them and wanted them to be saved. Like many young Christians, I had an abundance of enthusiasm. My grandparents knew that I spoke from a place of sincerity, that I was not being disrespectful because that was something I didn't do. Looking back, they could have interpreted that as being disrespectful, but Grandma understood I was sincere.

There was only one time my grandmother smacked me for asking a question disrespectfully, and that never happened again. I was a quick study, and I never wanted her to have that look of disappointment on her face again.

I was a junior counselor at a Christian camp, and that summer I learned so many Bible verses I almost didn't need a concordance! We had to memorize a Bible verse before we ate dinner every night. Frankly, I memorized them without knowing what they meant. But in later years when I went through rough times, those verses were in me and I started spewing them like a flood. What I had learned without understanding was available to me later when I needed it. I believe that God stored His Word in my heart then, and I can still quote those verses whenever I need them by His grace.

The Key to my Life

CHAPTER EIGHT

In New York City, the high school system works two ways: there are the local high schools that you go to based on your district, and there are specialized high schools that you can go to according to what you want to be. There's Music & Art High School, High School of the Performing Arts, Bronx High School of Science, Stuyvesant (for the brainiacs), various trade and technical high schools, and, for those who want to be engineers, there is Brooklyn Technical High School.

You have to pass an exam to get into Brooklyn Tech, and it was an hour and a half each way, bus and subway, from my grandparents' house. I was not afraid of the test, and that was where I wanted to go.

I took the test, and I told my grandmother how excited I was waiting for the results. "Renee, we need to get something straight right now. You are not about to get on buses and trains at no six in the morning to go to Brooklyn Tech."

"Huh? What are you talking about? That's where I want to go!" I would have gladly gotten up at four in the morning to go to that school.

"Let me explain something to you. I raised two children before you and your brother. I was younger then, and if there was a problem I could go and get them wherever they were in this city. But I'm older now. Grandma is Grandma, and I will never allow you to be in a position or a place where I can not get to you, and therefore I am telling you now that means your movements and where you go will be very limited. I am sorry, Renee, but I can't let you do that." I thought about what she said, and that there were a lot of things I would not be able to do that my friends would be doing. At the same time, I felt the love and concern. I understood completely what she was saying. I didn't like it, but I was happy to have a family. That might have bothered some other kids, but somehow I wasn't angry at all. I had to realize I had new borders and limits and I would get over not liking it. It was minor compared to having a home with people who love you and make you feel safe and secure. I was not heartbroken.

Grandma was serious, and I wasn't going to push it. Anytime I would ask my grandmother if I could go to an event, or a party, or wherever, she would say, "Imma sleep and pray on it and I'll let you know." That also meant having to ask way in advance if I wanted any chance of her considering my request, but that did not stop me from asking. And if it was in the evening, almost invariably she would come back and say, "No, you're not going." I wasn't ever happy about it, but I didn't get mad. I would always wonder why I couldn't go.

One time she had told me I could go to the park during the day with a bunch of other kids. I would be careful for sure, stay away from trouble, and the park was so close to the house. It was a community event in the South Ozone Park neighborhood and I had asked more than a week in advance. Then, the morning of the event, she said, "I'm sorry Renee, but I had to change my mind. You can't go."

As respectfully as I could, I said, "But Grandma, you said I could go."

"Sorry, Renee this is one of those things that I got a feeling about, and after sleeping on it and praying about it, you can't go, and that's the end of it." I was upset and sad. I called my girlfriend to tell her I wasn't going, and we were both furious and I still didn't go. I wasn't so angry later when we were told about the shooting in the park, in the place and at the time that I wanted to be there.

From that day on, I didn't question her, no matter how upset it made me. Whether or not she had a direct line to God, I wasn't taking a chance.

Toward the end of that summer, I received a letter from the Department of Education. It said that a high school very close to home, August Martin High School, was creating an Institute of Science and Technology that included engineering. It went on to say that my test scores from Brooklyn Tech made me an excellent candidate for their program, and extended an invitation to me to attend if I was interested. My grandmother suggested that I might want to get interested since the school was only a mile and a half away! She said I could go there!

It was a new program, a separate group of students within August Martin High School. We were treated as special, but the teachers also expected a lot from us. I was ready for this. They gave us aptitude tests, and mine came back "ENGINEER," which I expected. I had already done my research at the library; I knew the different fields of engineering, what the jobs were, how much they paid, and I was ready for that, too.

There was a class taught by Mr. Romano in aeronautical engineering that didn't fit my schedule, so I went to talk to Mr. Romano. "The only way you can fit this class in," he said, "would be to give up your lunch."

"I'll be there." I didn't care about lunch; I was checking all the boxes on my way to my goal. Renee's freight train was on the track.

In ninth grade, I met a girl named Leslie Gibson. We became best friends right away and stayed best friends through high school, college, and beyond. She invited me to her house one day, and this was one of the rare occasions where my grandmother said "Yes." And so I met the Gibson family. I immediately felt like I was in the presence of the perfect family. I immediately found a home with them, and they swiftly adopted me into the family.

Leslie was the youngest of three. She had an older brother, Phillip, and an older sister named Phyllis. Leslie's mother, Dorothy, was a registered nurse. Her dad, James, was a firefighter. This was a family! And I wanted to be part of it, so I kind of grafted onto the Gibsons. Fortunately, Mrs. Gibson was prudent. One day she took me home because she wanted to meet my grandmother. I didn't understand why, but she explained, "If you live with your grandmother and you're going to come over here, she's going to want to know who I am and who you're with."

So Mrs. Gibson met my grandmother and assured her that she could check up on me anytime I was at her house. Mrs. Gibson made herself accountable to my grandmother, which allowed the friendship between Leslie and me to grow. It also allowed me to become part of their family, which I loved, and which confirmed again my vision of a nuclear family that could be together and thrive.

Later in high school, while doing my constant career research to see what career would be the best and where I could make the most money, I learned about industrial management engineering, which combined engineering knowledge with business. My yearbook, which for the life of me I cannot find, says that I planned a career in industrial management engineering, and that has been my career since.

I also enjoyed playing varsity volleyball, singing in both chorus and jazz chorus, and I was a member of the Queensborough Community Chorus. I especially loved being voted Editor-in-Chief of my high school yearbook. They said they needed someone to do it and I was not shy. I was shining. I wasn't one of those kids who just "got through" high school; I discovered myself there. Between school and church, I was becoming the person God intended me to be, and I was loving it.

I still loved music. There was a soul station on AM radio in New York City, WWRL, all the way down at the end of the dial, where I listened to Ashford & Simpson (I listen to them to this day), Chaka Khan, and Earth, Wind & Fire. I got my first record player in high school, and I remember buying Stevie Wonder's *Songs In the Key of Life*, which is, in my opinion, still one of the best albums ever made. I also bought my first Ashford & Simpson LP. I wore that one out!

In my last year of high school, I had a very kind boyfriend. Vincent was only the second boyfriend I had in high school. He was a very nice guy, which was really what I needed. Of course, Grandpa Fletcher didn't want me dating, but I was 16 going on 17, and there were some half-days of school that my grandparents didn't know about when I would meet up with my friends. Vincent had gone away to college, so he was only around when he came home on holidays and a rare weekend or two. So I snuck around a little. There was not a whole lot of sneaking around in my world, because you can't sneak much when your folks are always home. Of course, my friends were sneaking around big time. I wasn't perfect, but I was a good girl. I sure tried for perfection, but I was a teenage girl in New York and I could keep knowledge of those half-days out of school from Grandma and Grandpa. And Vincent, being the good guy he was, volunteered to come and meet my grandparents. Of course, Grandpa gave him the third, fourth and fifth-degree, but he passed.

When I was applying to colleges, I learned that my SAT scores didn't put me on track for many engineering programs. I was receiving up to five applications a day, and one day I received an application from the University of Pittsburgh, which wasn't on my radar up to that point. "University of Pittsburgh!" Russell shouted, "Tony Dorsett goes to the University of Pittsburgh!" I'm not much of a sports person, but I'd heard of Tony Dorsett. "So?" I said. "So you should go there. And if you go there, I'll come visit." I filled out and sent the application. And then I got a letter from the University of Pittsburgh saying that they had an Engineering Impact program specifically for engineering students whose SATs or grades, one or the other, might be lacking. It was a six-week summer program that would lead up to their regular engineering program.

By the way, Russell never made good on his promise to come to visit during my four years at the University of Pittsburgh.

Another door was opening by God's grace, and I was ready to walk through. Whenever the time was right, God made the way, and always just in time.

Grit and Determination

CHAPTER NINE

Of course, I had to remember that I wasn't the only decision-maker when it came to my life. I showed the letter to my grandparents, hoping they would see the opportunity as I saw it. This program meant starting college early and staying with the program throughout my college career. Also, the program provided tutoring, counseling, and financial aid.

"You like this program? Is this what you want?" my grandfather asked. Of course it was. "Well, call the people."

I called the recruiter right away. Stewart Atwater was a congenial black man, helpful and friendly. My grandfather sat beside me as I spoke to Mr. Atwater on the phone. "Tell him you want to come visit."

Grandpa was still a warrior. Grandpa, Grandma, and I left the house at three in the morning and arrived at the University of Pittsburgh at about 10 am. I think we made one stop. Grandpa may have been just as excited as I was if that could have been possible.

As soon as I set my foot on that campus, I knew. I felt that this was right. I didn't need to see any more to make my decision--this was where I was going to college. But my grandfather made sure I checked all the boxes. "Take the tour, Renee. Have lunch here.

See the classrooms, the dorms, whatever." And so I did it all – but I knew. God was putting me there, and more than I knew then, He was giving me the desire of my heart.

My grandmother made it clear during the visit that they would have to find me a place in a dormitory if I was going to attend. She was adamant. I was not going to be living in an apartment or in any unsupervised arrangement. They must have known she wasn't bluffing – I sure did!

And then we were back in the car, and seven hours later we were back home – whoosh! That was my grandfather, doing it like we were driving uptown! Grandma had suggested getting a hotel, but Grandpa just did not see the need. On the way home, my grandmother and I talked about what I liked about the school, what I would need to go there, and more about why I wanted to go and what my hopes were.

The program started in June before my high school graduation. To attend graduation, I would have to miss a week of school in Pittsburgh. "I would like to go to my graduation," I told Mr. Atwater, "but I'm on a mission, and college is my priority." I was starting to see high school as chump change and the university as big money. I was out.

"Renee, the first week is only testing and introductory things," he answered. "We can get you squared away so you don't miss anything you need. You've worked hard in high school; please go to your graduation."

It was surprisingly easy for me to walk away from high school. I had been active in school; I played volleyball and was editor-in-chief of the yearbook. I was first-runner-up for homecoming queen, and I had loved going to August Martin. But I was done. I was ready to move on to bigger and better. There were really no goodbyes to be said. I was facing forward and looking toward completing the engineering pre-college program, and I was determined to matriculate to the School of Engineering.

Grandpa also had a plan. "We'll go to your graduation with the car packed and ready. You graduate and we'll hit the road." That was a great decision because despite my feelings at the time. I'm glad I was able to attend graduation with my best friend Leslie, get our diplomas, and have a proper goodbye. She was the only person I needed or wanted to say goodbye to.

Of course, there were some obstacles at the beginning of my college career. There was some difficulty finding me a dorm room, which would have meant that I wouldn't have been able to attend. Fortunately, because I was in the engineering summer program, the director of the engineering department was able to get me a single room in the nurses' residence hall, which was just across the street from the engineering school. Being that close and not having a roommate kept me laser-focused on my studies. It was a perfect arrangement, and somehow I was able to keep the single room and stay in that building for my entire four years of college.

They gave us a speech at the beginning of the semester, a fairly common speech: "Look to your left and look to your right – only one of you will be here in four years." That was supposed to be encouraging? It's a fear tactic; I just felt sorry for the other two people in this statistic, because I was going to be the one who made it. I knew then that it wasn't about statistics; it was about making a decision, and I had already made mine.

I had to up my game significantly in terms of studying. Many of the engineering students had already taken classes that I would need. I also needed to build new habits and shift the schedule I had been living for years. Instead of fitting my studies around my household chores, I had to fit everything else around my studies. And I discovered that being at the top of my class in high school didn't translate to college. This was going to take a lot of work.

The university was also my introduction to something I had not experienced as a New York City kid: real racism. However hard I dug in, there was the feeling of being "other." There were constant reminders, including a few professors who told me that I shouldn't be there, that I was in the wrong place with the wrong background, and that "people like me" wouldn't finish the engineering program. They were talking to the wrong girl, but that didn't make it any easier.

During my junior and senior years in the school of engineering, I had the opportunity to be part of a great study group. There were four of us in the group, all women: Carolyn (or 'Lee Lee' as we affectionately called her), Nancy, and Lora (all of whom were white), and me. These women were a great support group as we all studied and did our industrial engineering senior team project together. They had the up-close opportunity to see and share my struggles to earn great grades, especially with how exams were graded differently based on the subjective opinion of the professor.

All of the other ladies in the group had very good to excellent grades, but not me. I remember one time we were all studying together as usual and we were reviewing our grades on one test. I had gotten a C and the others had earned As and a B+. One of the ladies asked me for my exam. "Let's see what happened here. We all know this material." She was going over the test question by question when I saw a startled look on her face. She said that we had made the same math errors, but where she received a 1-5 point deduction, my deductions were 15-20 points.

All my study partners suggested that I go to the professor and say something. I explained to my friends that speaking out would not solve the problem. In fact, as the only black person in our class, it would shine more light on me and put me under more scrutiny than I thought I could stand.

Ultimately, I did go to the professor intending to ask him about each question and why he took off so many points for my math errors. He said he believed I didn't understand how to solve the problem and that he took off fewer points for those he thought understood how to solve the problem. So, somehow my error was a result of not understanding, but for others, an error was due to a miscalculation (because he believed they understood the material), and that resulted in a minor deduction. It was a frustration I was willing to bear because it was my reality and I was determined to graduate. Situations like that just added fuel to my engine and helped me to continue to move forward. It was just another reason for me to dig in and graduate. They say success is the best revenge; of course, it has a cost which might be one's mental health.

So I didn't have the college experience some people had. I didn't party--I studied. I didn't hang out--I worked. I felt like I was in a struggle for my life, an uphill climb to make it through college. I fought through the intense workload for every single grade, and even then my grades were not great, but I persevered. I was determined and extremely focused. Nothing - and I mean *nothing* - was going to turn me around. Renee's freight train climbed some steep hills during those years, and when I graduated, I celebrated. I graduated in August because I needed a couple of classes at the end.

College had been exhausting, and before I could enter the corporate world, I needed a mental break. I took Stewart Atwater's job for a year and recruited others into the engineering program, giving students like me a chance to achieve. As always, there was nothing wasted.

My extreme mental anguish and exhaustion from some of the treatment at school moved me to work in recruiting other students into the program that allowed me to become an engineer.

Grandpa's Hand

I met the man who would become my husband after a few months at college. We clicked as friends right away. Dwayne was the first person I ever told my whole story to, and I didn't know why in the world I felt comfortable enough with this guy to tell him all this.

He was amazed that I had been through all I had been through and could still be so strong and together. I know God put us together, and Dwayne told me a long time later that he had always felt, on some level, that it was his role to take care of me. He said that even at the start when we were just friends he knew that his calling was to be there for me, and he consciously prepared for that mission. He spoke those sentiments again when we renewed our vows during our 30th wedding anniversary ceremony.

Even as we grew closer in college, I told him, "I am here to go to college, I'm not looking for a husband or anything like that." I had made my grandfather a promise that I would not get married until I had graduated from college, and I was not going to break that promise. I would never break my word to my grandparents, and never dishonor my grandfather. "I don't need a relationship; I need a diploma."

"Cool," Dwayne said. It didn't exactly work out like that, but that was the initial agreement. By the end of that first year, we were definitely in love, and we were together throughout college. But I kept my promise.

The standards my grandparents set for me kept the "Renee Train" on track. I had the drive and ambition, but with the freedom of college, I could have easily gone off if it weren't for their teaching, the principles I learned from them, and the guidelines they set for me. And the guiding principle that drove my behavior, and still does to this day, is that I have always wanted my decisions and my life to reflect the sacrifice my grandparents made, and for them to be proud and smile at the way I live my life.

God sets it all in motion, puts the people and events in place, and it all works together if we let it. And I am so grateful that my grandparents taught me the things I needed to stay out of my own way.

Dwayne met my grandparents at the end of my freshman year. I remember that so well - this big, young, football-player-looking guy standing with my short, military-bearing grandfather. Grandpa looked up into Dwayne's eyes and said, "Negro, you don't scare me." We all burst out laughing.

"What are you about, young man?" Grandpa asked. "Our Renee is about everything. What are you about?" I don't remember what Dwayne answered, but it must have been good because he passed the test.

After Dwayne asked me three times to marry him, we got engaged at the end of my junior year. To be clear, we *planned* to get engaged, and Dwayne said he was going to come to New York and ask my grandfather. "I know," Dwayne told me, "that that is what I have to do." I just nodded "Yes." Grandpa had made it clear that nothing was going to happen without his approval.

We arrived at my grandparents' house on a Friday evening. Saturday morning, Grandma had me up at 7 am to meet Aunt Sandra and "go do a few things." We were going to look at wedding dresses, but since Dwayne hadn't spoken to Grandpa yet, we were just going to do a few things. Grandma knew already, but I took my grandfather's approval so seriously I wasn't sure it was appropriate to even go looking yet!

It was always clear that, although she didn't argue with Grandpa (at least not that anyone else ever saw), she did have his ear. So my grandmother saw that the deal as done, even though I was awaiting my grandfather's endorsement.

We left the house. Dwayne was up and sitting in the living room waiting for my grandfather. He knew Grandpa was military, and he wanted to be up and waiting. Dwayne told me that my grandfather smiled when he entered – he knew what Dwayne was doing and he respected it.

"Come on, let's go," Grandpa said to Dwayne. He led Dwayne to the car. They got in, and Grandpa drove to the nearby neighborhood of Jamaica Estates (you may have seen Jamaica Estates in the movie *Coming To America*).

Jamaica Estates was, for us, where the people who made it lived. The Trumps lived in Jamaica Estates. Successful, rich, Black people lived in Jamaica Estates.

"Look around," my grandfather said. "This is what Renee ought to have. Renee deserves the best and this is how she should be living. If this is not what you're about, if you're not after the best life, please leave her alone. She doesn't need anything less than this, and she can do it all on her own."

Grandpa gave his approval that day. After that conversation, he gave Dwayne his blessing to marry me.

When Dwayne told me about their conversation later, I felt so good that my grandfather acknowledged that I was valued, that I was amazing, and that I deserved the best! And Grandpa didn't change that tune even up to the wedding: he was holding Dwayne's feet to the fire. "You don't impress me. Don't tell me--show me what you're going to do for Renee."

Dwayne graduated the year before I did, and after I got my diploma, we got married. The wedding was on August 31st, only weeks after I graduated and completed all classes to become an industrial engineer. I know God put us together and directed us to wait. And I know that one of the things He made us wait for was my grandfather's approval.

The family came to Pittsburgh for our wedding, and my grandfather took my hand and looked at Dwayne and me and said, "You're in good hands now. You two are good, and I am, too."

Four months later, in December, Grandpa Fletcher passed. He wasn't sick, never broke stride. He walked into the kitchen one day and fell dead on the floor. My grandmother told me he was ready because he knew I was good, that I was settled, and all was well.

It was as if he had been waiting for me to be okay.

Dwayne told me that he had been looking forward to maybe going fishing with my grandfather. He felt that they had been cheated of some beautiful grandfather-in-law moments, but I am grateful for the way he died; my grandfather was a man with great dignity, and I thank God he didn't have to waste away in a sickbed. I think he would have been saddened, embarrassed. He went exactly the way he wanted to go.

The Gift of Love Returned

I stayed with my grandmother for a few weeks after Grandpa's funeral, and it was during that time that Grandma started to open up to me as one adult to another. My grandparents had never tried to act young or to relate to my brother and I as equals.

They were *grandparents* and they thrived in that position. But once I was married and the grandparent role had been fulfilled, the relationship began to expand. She had saved my life, given Russell and me a home and family, and I cannot express the depth of my love, and especially my respect, for my grandmother. And now I was grown, and Grandma told me things she had never told me before: how she and Grandpa met, how some of her friends that I thought were married weren't, and it just got honest and real between us as grownups.

She even shared with me that she felt she hadn't been a good mother to my dad and my aunt – how could she have been a good mother if she raised the person that was my father? She had seen herself as a failure, especially after Dad had put us in a home.

I had always seen her as the best parent and grandparent anyone could have. Maybe she hadn't done so well with her son, or even her daughter (who I idolized), but to me, she had always been sure-footed and confident in her parenting. She had always acted as though she had done all this before and she knew what worked. I believe she saw an opportunity in raising Russell and me, a do-over, another chance to get it right.

How could I tell my grandmother how perfect she was for us, how she had gotten it right with us? I had to make sure she would know, so I put it in a letter. Writing letters was how my Grandmother taught me to communicate with her, and when something was important, we made sure we put everything down on paper to fully express our feelings and thoughts. This was one of the most brilliant lessons she instilled in me--the gift of writing and the ability to communicate my feelings through writing.

This was the last written exchange we shared. In this letter, I told her I loved her, and from the depths of my soul, I wrote that she was everything to us, that she had rescued us, and most importantly, she had never once let us down. We spoke about it and she sent me a letter, too. It was our way. I thank God that I had the opportunity to give at least that much to my wonderful grandmother.

We had a special connection. It was a remarkable gift that I had never been aware of before my grandfather passed, but for the rest of her life, I was constantly aware of her love and her presence. And the fact that there was one person in the world who could see me just as I am has allowed me to become all that I have become.

Grandma had a stroke in 2001. She recovered, but some things changed in her manner, mainly her attitude and her desire to live life to the fullest. She became very apprehensive and didn't want to go anywhere or do much of anything. That very spunky, stylish, fun person died with the stroke. Aunt Sandra tried to take care of her for a time, but she was reaching the point where she couldn't do it anymore. I told my aunt, "When you feel like you can't take care of her anymore, put Grandma on a plane and send her to me."

I told my grandmother that she would always have a place with us, although I knew she didn't want to leave her home. Eventually, Aunt Sandra just became worn out and put her on that plane. I don't judge my aunt; she did all she could, and more importantly, she knew when she was done. Grandma came to Atlanta where Dwayne and I had moved and lived with us.

I think the change that startled me the most was that my grandmother, the sure-footed guide of my life, gave up making decisions. "I'm done making decisions, Renee," she said to me. "From now on, you do it. I am not making another decision." I took that one with a large grain of salt, until one day in the doctor's office when the doctor offered options for her care and asked how she wanted to proceed. Grandma turned to me and said, "Renee, tell him what I want to do. I told you, I'm done." She had genuinely checked out.

We spent many of Grandma's last days going back and forth to the hospital. My husband and I spent many days at the hospital because of the various medical complications my Grandmother had. We called 911 and went to the hospital often several times a month. We knew several of the nurses by their first names, and they would joke with me about my hoop earrings and my fashion sense. Even the ambulance drivers' faces became familiar after a while, and I was grateful for the chance to serve my grandmother.

After one hospitalization, Grandma went into a nursing home after leaving the hospital so she could have daily physical therapy. She had given up walking, too. My role had changed, and I became so sad watching this wonderful woman giving up and dying. Even so, she lived with us for seven years. Seven years of being ready to go and not going, of being gone and still there.

Dwayne and I were able to care for her until she died in 2010. God allowed me, with help from in-home hospice care, to take care of the woman who had taken such good care of me. To the end, her face lit up when she saw me, I became for her what she had always been for me. What a blessed opportunity. Again, nothing wasted; the trauma of my childhood and the blessing of being raised by my grandparents set me up to be willing and ready for the privilege and honor of opening my home to my Grandmother. I had the opportunity to love and care for her as she did for me and my brother.

My husband was 100% all in. Dwayne is the youngest of eight and understands family better than most people. I could not have asked for a better partner or a more willing participant. At this same time, his mother was sick and under care in Virginia. We would visit her as often as we could. Our younger daughter Dominique received her calling to a nursing career thanks to her young lifetime of helping to care for both of her grandmothers. The family unit living in our home worked as a team to take care of Grandma; my cousin, Merle, had experience as a certified nursing assistant and caregiver and was extremely helpful in showing us what to do. Many times she took the lead in providing care. Dominique spent all of her free time in the room with Grandma. She loved talking with her, getting the things she needed, and just being in her presence. She never wanted to go anywhere or doing anything else, just sit in the room with Grandma. Courtney and Cousin Eddie were also part of the family team, jumping in when needed to make sure Grandma was loved and cared for as well. We also had great caregivers for Grandma who were like family. Tatie, on the front end of Grandma's time with us, stayed with us for a few years. Later we had Sheila, who spent the last years of Grandma's life as her caregiver.

The hospice people were there for her, too, at the end. When they came to help, they had asked us what our wishes were regarding my grandmother's passing, and I had told them that it would be better if she didn't pass away at home. I had been thinking about how busy the house was, how many people, and what it would mean for us to become a house of mourning.

One November day about ten in the morning, the hospice caregiver came downstairs to me and said, "It's time." I just looked at her. "I can call now," she said, "and we can take her."

"Wait a minute," I said, feeling it in my gut. "Can't we just see if she's really ready…"

"Ms. Bradford, we want to abide by your wishes. You told us you didn't want your grandmother to pass away at your house. If that's still true, we need to move her today." I believe the main reason I didn't want Grandma to transition in the house was that Dominique was still at home, and I did not want her to look at the house or that room as the place where Nana died. I could also feel my own denial wrestling with what I was being told.

I asked the lady, "Can you have the ambulance come at seven this evening?"

"They will be here at seven," she answered flatly. I realized that this woman did not think my grandmother would live to see 7:00.

By this time, my aunt Sandra, my brother Russell, and other family members had all moved to the Atlanta area. I got on the phone and told them all, "If you want to see Grandma before she goes into hospice, come on over."

Everyone came and stayed until the ambulance came and took her to the hospice location. My grandmother hung on for about a week before she passed.

I had already grieved because the Grandma who raised me had died a long time before. The rest of the family had to go through the process, but I was able to move on to the joy of knowing that we had had our time together, that I was given the gift of being able to do for her what she had done for me. There were no regrets, no "I shoulda woulda..." because I had done it and it had all come full circle. I was proud and grateful for what my family had be-come--grateful to God, and grateful to my grandmother.

Faith Not Wasted

CHAPTER TWELVE

After 12 years in Pittsburgh, Dwayne and I were led to move to Alpharetta, Georgia, outside of Atlanta, to raise our family. As much as I am a New York City girl (and always will be), and as much as I love my hometown, it's a blessing that my children grew up in an environment where they were able to see successful people that looked like them in various professions and roles.

They grew up seeing and knowing that they could achieve anything because they had visual proof. There were also many career opportunities in the South, so moving to Atlanta had always been a goal for us.

Our home is large and open, and we've been fortunate enough to welcome other family members. One of our cousins who lived in New Jersey told us she was worried about her son, Eddie, growing up around gangs. Eddie came to us for the summer, and Dwayne and I decided to ask my cousin to let Eddie live with us. "Life is good here, the house is big, and our girls would have a big brother." My cousin Merle gave it some thought and said, "Yeah, why not? And I'm coming, too!"

It was Dwayne and me, our two daughters, my grandmother, my cousin, and her son. And I was in my glory because I had this house running like a well-oiled machine. All the things my grandfather taught me, along with any natural organizational ability I might have had, came into play. Nothing in my life has been wasted, and all things have come together for the good.

Sunday has been my day of worship and cooking. I cooked for the week because three kids taking lunches meant a lot of meal prep. Eight people were living in my house, which fluctuated to nine or more at some point. My mother's lesson of laying out clothes on the chair wasn't wasted, either--the children laying out their clothes the night before became the rule of the house. Actually, they laid out five outfits for the week on Sunday night.

I could not have been more blessed running this house all these years. We raised two daughters, cared for my grandmother, had my cousins here, and did all this because of God's grace and the lessons of everything that has happened in my life. Grandma used to say, "If you want something done, give it to a busy person," and I love being that person.

The opportunity to be busy, to be efficient, has given me joy. When I have been in that zone, God has provided me with the ability to do it all seamlessly to the point where I've made it appear flawless. I praise God for this accomplishment, all done in His strength, and with His grace.

My older daughter, Courtney, graduated from Columbia University Law School and works as an attorney with a firm in New York City.

My younger daughter, Dominique (who we affectionately call "Nikki"), was diagnosed with receptive expressive language disorder, a developmental condition. Watching her grow and seeing her achieve milestones and miracles along the way kept us on our knees. Helping her grandmothers gave her a dream of going into nursing despite being told she didn't have the abilities. Dwayne's sister LaVerne and her husband Dallas took Nikki back to Virginia to live with them, and LaVerne researched nursing programs. She was able to enroll Nikki in the same program in Virginia that she had attended. It also helped that LaVerne knew the instructor.

At first, we couldn't figure out how she was going to succeed. My husband said he would take a leave of absence from his work to accompany Nikki to classes and study with her every night. Dwayne is a resolute man. He meant it, and he would have gladly done it, but God had it covered. He did it through LaVerne and Dallas, who provided the rigorous schedule and structure that enabled Nikki to thrive and succeed. In that clinical nursing assistant program, my daughter was earning As while we were thinking we'd have to figure out how she was going to pass. She excelled for the duration of the program and maintained great grades. She even passed her in-person exam on her first attempt.

My nephew Eddie, who came to live with us when he was in seventh grade, initially had a hard time reading. Dwayne read with him, made him read aloud, and encouraged him to not give up. My nephew graduated from Morehouse College and Morehouse School of Medicine. Today he is an ophthalmologist on staff at a major hospital.

I managed my home, but God has always been in charge. As long as we have been about His business, He has been deeply involved in ours.

At one point, Dwayne and I started a restaurant business and, unfortunately, we lost every single dime we had. Not to mention we had a house full of people to support.

"Lord," I said, "How can You do this to us?"

"That's not one of those Bible verses of yours," Dwayne said. I just couldn't understand how we could be going down that way.

I was terrified.

One morning we had the TV on and I was just crying. I went off into another room to pray. "God, I've got a house full of people and no money. I am so scared. You've gotta tell us what to do. I know I'm missing something. Tell me what we need to do." I went back to the living room and Creflo Dollar was on the TV. He talked about a Bible study they were doing that day. Dwayne had to go and get the restaurant ready to close down. I said, "I'm going to that Bible study."

Dwayne nodded and said, "Go. Represent us."

I went to the church. I prayed to God again. And again. The preacher doing the Bible study got up. "I had my study all prepared last night," he said, "and then God woke me up and told me I needed to preach on fear."

He preached a study with ten Bible verses about coping with fear. It all came down to this: faith abolishes fear – the more faith, the less fear. I wrote down the ten things with tears streaming down my face. When I got home, I read them all to Dwayne.

The message in that Bible study that day convinced us, beyond a doubt, that God's Word is to be believed. How did I come to a place where a preacher changed his message the night before to be just what I needed that day?

Now, when I say we lost every dime, I mean there were times when Dwayne and I looked at each other over a $5 bill, not knowing how we would get through the week. And then, looking at God's Word, somehow I was able to go into Walmart with $35 and feed our eight-person household for a week. Dwayne and I wish we could do that today! But a miracle is a miracle, and that was grace like manna from Heaven.

Dwayne and I have dived into the pool of God's Word and we are not coming up. Oh, we have our moments, but everything, always, points us back to Him. One of the decisions we made during that time was that we would not speak anything but what God would have us speak, and that we would not ever complain no matter what came our way. No matter how bad it got, we either spoke good or we were quiet.

Somehow we didn't have to go bankrupt. Instead, we went to work! Dwayne got a second job and so did I. We worked things out to pay our creditors. Within six months I was back to my old income.

I don't have my notes from that study anymore – I later gave them to someone who needed them, my friend Treza. She and her then-husband Eddie are like family, brother and sister to us. Their son had a brain tumor. They called us on the day he was diagnosed and admitted to the hospital. I went immediately to be by their side, taking my notebook with the "Ten Reasons Not To Fear" written inside. When I got there, Treza, her cousin Pat, and I were in the room.

This was a rare occasion where the power of God was immediately palpable to me. I began to share the Word, what I had learned about why we should not fear. Pat began to chime in with each reason, and then we all grabbed hands and begin to pray for her son with gratitude and full belief in God and what He would do.

I realized then that my circumstance of losing everything and having God show up for me at the right moment with that teaching about fear was meant for me to learn and share with Treza. He selected me to help her and Eddie by sharing an example of God's grace and goodness during their son's heroic battle with a brain tumor. Once more, a demonstration of how nothing is wasted. Her son lived on for another year or so, touching many lives. His life moved many prayer groups to lift him and his family in prayer. He accomplished his mission in this life, and we know for sure we will see him again and celebrate at the Pearly Gates.

I have never believed that God just drops goodness out of the sky, and I still believe that I need to work for what I want in this world. But He has given my family and me so much--so many blessings, many of which did not look like blessings when they first appeared. He's bestowed so many blessings that I can't count them all.

I don't worry anymore. I believe. We started over and trusted Him. When we can't see what's over the next hill, we trust Him. And it's always goodness.

This little girl who watched her mother dragged off in a straitjacket, who was pushed into Social Services' care and told by her father that nobody wanted her is now a strong black woman who has been given the grace to use everything that has ever happened—EVERYTHING--to build this life. Not a single event, or even a single moment, has been wasted. All things have, indeed, worked together for my good.

You're Free

About ten years ago, I decided to find my father. My daughter Courtney was headed to Columbia University for basketball camp, as she was considering matriculating there. She and I were going to fly to New York City, so the time seemed right.

I reached out to my sister. Mikole and I communicate regularly – in fact, we are best friends today. One of the greatest blessings in my life is having an amazing relationship with Mikole, and we worked for every bit of it! She has become my biggest fan, and has always given me so much love and warmth every time we have gotten together. Once we grew up and could create a sisterhood of our own, we did just that. I cherish my sister and our relationship. Since I had to wait until we were in a place in our lives where we could create the bond we have, I am so very grateful for her and her love. None of the difficult and beautiful work we've put into this connection will ever be wasted because we created and carved out this precious sisterhood.

So I called my sister and told her I was coming up and she invited me to hang out with her for a few days. I said, "You know what, Mikole? I would really like to find Daddy."

She hadn't seen him in about ten years; I hadn't seen him in over 20. She said she wanted to find him, too. I think we had different motives but the same desire. Dad had spent many more years with Mikole and her mom than he had with me, so she knew a very different man.

I knew only one way to track down my father. I asked Aunt Sandra, and she agreed to begin the search and put the word out that we were looking for him. "I can always find him," she said, and she always could. She called back with his last known address, and now we had a plan.

Then Courtney surprised me. She asked, "Can you please wait so I can come with you to find my grandfather?" At first I wasn't sure. But something prompted me to say "Okay." I mean, why not? He's her grandfather.

So we went to the address, which was located in a housing project: my sister, my daughter, my cousin Kia, and me. We went up in the funky-smelling elevator in the projects and knocked on the door. A woman's voice came through the door: "Hello?"

"Hello, is Russell Burke here?"

The lady's voice became really nervous, almost angry. "Who's that? Who are you? What do you want?"

My sister answered softly, "This is his daughter, Mikole. Does Russell live here?"

There was a pause, followed by a sound that's familiar to any New York City apartment dweller: a series of latches and locks being unlatched and unlocked. The door opened. None of us had ever seen this woman before.

"You're Mikole?" She paid no attention to the rest of us. "Okay, I know where your father is. I'll take you to him, but then I'm gonna run. I don't want him to see that it was me that brought you there."

We all got back into the funky-smelling New York projects elevator, and then the woman turned to me and said, "You must be Renee." I nodded. She said, "You're as beautiful as I thought you would be."

We walked two blocks until we were across the street from a little bodega with a bunch of men sitting in lawn chairs in front. She pointed to a man who was getting out of his chair to go into the store. "That's your dad...see you!" She turned and started running back the way we came.

We were crossing the street when my cousin said, "Wait. Wait until he comes out of the bodega."

"Right," I answered. "That's a small store. We don't want him to feel trapped, you know?"

We waited. He came out of the store and started walking up the block. I called out, "Mike!" Mike was my father's nickname because there were so many Russells in the family when he was coming up. He stopped and turned. We came up to him. "Do you know who we are?" He looks. Looks again. "No."

"We're your daughters."

He collapsed to the ground. We held him up as he muttered, "Oh my God...oh my God." Some young brother came out of the bodega and got between us and asked my father if he was okay, if we were doing something to him. I started laughing at what it must look like. "No, I'm fine," my father said as he regained his footing.

"You sure?" the young man said. "Nah, really, I'm good." The young guy backed off.

"Daddy, I'm Renee."

"I know who you are."

"Well, before we go further, your mother lives with me and she wants to speak to you." Grandma was still alive at this point, but very sickly. "She's not always 'with it,' but she wants to talk to you." I called her right there. Merle was at home with her, and thankfully she was pretty lucid. They spoke for a few minutes. I could only hear his side of course, but they got to talk, which was my grandmother's wish.

After they spoke, I introduced him to my daughter. "Do you know who this is?" I asked.

"This must be my granddaughter. I know, 'cause she looks just like your mother." He said she looked exactly like my mother did when they were dating. Not close, not a striking resemblance, but exactly.

He asked about my brother. "Russell's not married, is he?" I shook my head. "He doesn't have children, does he?"

"No," I answered.

"He has a lot of problems, right?"

"Yeah, he's just like me. And he's still mad at me, huh?"

"Uh-huh," I said. I didn't tell him that Russell had said that if he saw our father again, he'd kill him.

But I hadn't yet done what I came to do. As we walked my father back to the projects, I said, "Daddy, I came here for one reason. I'm here to let you know that you are free. There is no condemnation. I've never been mad at you and I'm not mad at you now."

He just stopped and looked at me.

"You probably think I might be angry," I said, "But I want you to know that you're free. Free. If you thought there was something bad between us, I forgive you. I love you and you don't owe me a thing. We can start from right now. My life has been rich and beautiful.

"You might look at what you did as bad, but for me, it was the best thing you could have done. Because I am living my best life. You are forgiven. The past is past."

He kept walking. I must have told him four times that he was free and forgiven. He didn't acknowledge even that he had heard me. I told him again.

We walked to my sister's car. I had said what I came to say, so I got in the car while Mikole said her goodbyes.

My dad came over to the side of the car and motioned for me to roll my window down. "Renee," he said, "I heard what you said."

"Did you really, Daddy? Did you hear me tell you you're free? The only one who can keep you caged now is you. You. Are. Forgiven."

"I hear you," he said, "But I don't know if I can receive that. You're beautiful, and I thank you, but I don't know if I can take forgiveness."

"It's your choice, Dad. I came to set you free and now you decide what to do with it. I love you and I always will. And God loves you, too."

I got to see my father twice more in the ten years since that day. Then, on Good Friday of 2021, he called me. "How are you? How's Dwayne? How are your daughters?" It was the first time he spoke to me without starting with an apology. He called like a dad and we had an ordinary conversation! I am certain that he finally got it.

My mother was released from the hospital at some point while I was growing up and lived on disability. She was always dependent financially. We lived in a cycle. She was on medicine that she needed to take at all times, but she took it when she was sick and as soon as she felt better, she would go off her medication. Eventually I'd get a call from the New York City Police Department because she would be wandering around paranoid. From afar, I became her partial caregiver. My brother wanted nothing to do with any of it. It took many years to get her into a program with supervision, but after much work, and more than 20 years on waiting lists, we got her into a living situation where she shares an apartment, but the entire building is supervised and she has to take her meds every day. And then, a few years ago, she decided she didn't need to talk to me anymore. She called and said so, that she wouldn't be talking to me for a while. That didn't bother me at all - I knew she was dealing with her challenges, and as long as she was cared for, safe, and thriving, it was all fine with me. I don't take any of these changes personally or even as something to be sad about.

About a year ago, she sent me a letter telling me she was searching for me! She had forgotten our conversation completely. And we picked up where we left off, and now we talk periodically.

I am happy she's happy. Her social worker calls me from time to time.

This is the life I've chosen. I'm happy. God has given me my best life, and I share it as best I can.

As I read through this book, there's a song that keeps playing in my heart: Kurt Carr's *For Every Mountain*. I hope you'll listen to it and see if it resonates for you, too.

I hope that this story provides some hope, some joy, and some faith because that is the story of my life. Everything in it has been for the glory of God, and not a single moment has been wasted.

Acknowledgements

Heavenly Father, I thank you and I stand in awe of you and how you love each and every one of us and have loved me so much that you always created good and great from experiences and events that were terrible situations and tragedies in my life.

And I'm even more thankful that I can recognize the beauty from the ashes as rain falls on the just and unjust. The beauty is when we are in fellowship with you, and you take those situations and turn them into victories and triumph by allowing us to follow that great thought and plan you have for our lives.

Dear Lord, I thank you for Dwayne, my amazing husband, my best friend, confidant, my encourager, my rock. Thank you for giving us the strength to form such an amazing partnership, relationship, and marriage; our marriage is a ministry. Dwayne is truly a reflection of your heart and love!

Thank you for choosing me to be the mother for Courtney and Dominique. I consider it an honor that you chose me to be the vessel and the person to guide them on the pathway to the great plans you have for their lives. When they call me Mommy, I feel so blessed and honored. I know what a blessing being called Mommy is, and every time they say it, it warms my heart and soul.

Thank you for my beautiful sister, Mikole. From the moment I saw her I felt pure joy! I cherish and treasure our unbreakable bond and the amazing relationship we built together through work and love!

Thank you for Jeanette, my Mommy who was the absolute best mom to me; who exposed me to all of the beauty and culture that New York had to offer, especially the arts. Who showed me with her presence and being what a beautiful women looks like and is.

Thank you for the angels you placed in my life. Thank you for Mrs. Banks and her entire family who enveloped us with love. She was and is the most amazing angel for me who emanated and radiated love to me and my brother, Russell, at the most difficult time in our lives as children. Words cannot express the level of love and care she showed to us.

Thank you for my grandparents, Irene and Fletcher, who stopped everything in their lives to parent me and my brother with excellence and intention, and most of all love. They always made me feel loved and wanted, and they always told me that my brother and I coming into their lives made their lives richer and better, and they were the blessed ones. Wow!

Thank you for my mother-in-law, Betty, who was my mother-in-love. Actually, she was a mother to me for sure, and you, dear God, knew I needed that love. She welcomed me into her life with so much love and respect and humor; she was amazingly funny. She always saw something special in me, and was more than delighted to make me her daughter way before I married Dwayne. And she taught and mentored me as a women, wife, and mother.

Thank you for the beautiful friends who showed me what unconditional love looks like; my sister and friend, Sheila Robinson, who always exudes love and who was and is always right by my side, a true reflection of God. My best friend from high school, Leslie, who invited me into her family and shared her amazing parents with me.

Thank you for choosing Trudy to guide me on this part of the journey; that you chose to be that sister who I could be accountable to and show me the way by how she opens her home and heart up to everyone she meets with her smile and the heart of Christ, and her beautiful spirit and candor.

Made in the USA
Columbia, SC
07 June 2023

17534067R00054